ACCOUNTABILITY BUDDY
JOURNAL

A MINDFUL JOURNEY
THROUGH MY WEEKLY GOALS

CREATED BY KAYLIE FINNIS

ACCOUNTABILITY BUDDY
JOURNAL

CONCEPT & DESIGN CREATED IN NEW ZEALAND 2020
FIRST PUBLISHED BY KAYLIE FINNIS / LIQUID MANA LLC
DESIGN AND LAYOUT COPYRIGHT © KAYLIE FINNIS

KAYLIE FINNIS ASSERTS THE MORAL RIGHT TO BE IDENTIFIED AS THE AUTHOR OF THIS WORK.
ISBN 978-0-473-55637-2

KINDLY RECYCLE THIS BOOK AND PAGES INSTEAD OF DISPOSING OF THEM
PRINTED ON DEMAND, ON PAPER CHOSEN FOR BEING CONSCIOUS OF ENVIRONMENTAL IMPACT

WELCOME TO YOUR NEW ACCOUNTABILITY BUDDY!

TABLE OF CONTENTS

BONUS CONTENT

THE WHY

GAIN MOTIVATION

FORM NEW HABITS

SHAKE OLD HABITS

GET INSPIRED

INSPIRE OTHERS

OVERCOME FEARS AND HURDLES

GET STUFF DONE

HOW THIS WORKS

BEGINNING OF THE WEEK

1. SET YOUR INTENTION & FOCUS FOR THE WEEK

2. PICK 1-4 GOALS PER CATEGORY AND # OF DAYS/7

3. TAKE 2 MINUTES MORNING & NIGHT TO TRACK PROGRESS

END OF THE WEEK

1. REVIEW YOUR WEEK & ANSWER A FEW THOUGHTFUL QUESTIONS

2. OUTLINE NEXT WEEK'S INTENTION, FOCUS & GOALS

3. OPTIONAL: SEND A PIC OF THIS WEEK/NEXT WEEK TO YOUR BUDDY

BONUS CONTENT

MY ACCOUNTABILITY BUDDY ASKED ME FOR SOME PLANNING TOOLS

SO... AT THE BACK OF THE JOURNAL ARE SOME BLUEPRINTS

TO HELP YOU MAP OUT 12 MONTH AND 90 DAY GOALS

FURTHER INSPIRATION CAN BE ACHIEVED
IF YOU SHARE YOUR WEEK WITH
AN ACCOUNTABILITY BUDDY OR GROUP!

ACCOUNTABILITY IDEAS

INSPIRE SOMEONE
WRITE MORNING AFFIRMATIONS
SPENDING BUDGET FOR THE DAY/WEEK
GET OUTSIDE
NO SOCIAL MEDIA
NO TV/MOVIES
READ A REAL BOOK
PLAY MUSIC
LISTEN TO A PODCAST
ORGANISE/TIDY UP
DE-CLUTTER DIFFERENT ROOMS
NOTICE/BE MINDFUL OF MY THOUGHTS
PLAN WORKOUT CALENDAR
MEET A FRIEND FOR COFFEE
TRY OR DO A NEW ACTIVITY
GET A MASSAGE
TAKE A NAP
COLD WAKEUP SHOWER
WRITE A LETTER TO FRIEND OR FAMILY
CALL SOMEONE IN NEED OF CHEERING UP
DO SOMETHING YOU'VE BEEN AVOIDING
STUDY OR LEARN SOMETHING NEW
WRITE A POEM

ACCOUNTABILITY IDEAS

DRINK MORE WATER

GET MORE SLEEP

FLOSS MY TEETH

YOGA OR STRETCH

CARDIO

WEIGHTS/WORK OUT

BIKE/WALK/JOG/RUN

NO ALCOHOL DAYS

NO SUGAR DAYS

REDUCE CAFFEINE INTAKE

WEEKLY MEAL PREP/PLANNING

COOK DINNER AT HOME

MAKE A HEALTHY BREAKFAST

HAVE A GREEN JUICE OR SMOOTHIE

MAKE A SALAD

DO SOME ART/SOMETHING CREATIVE

WRITE 3 THINGS I'M GRATEFUL FOR

WRITE 3 THINGS I WANT TO HAPPEN

WRITE IN A JOURNAL FOR 15 MINUTES

MEDITATE OR SIT IN SILENCE

SPEND TIME IN MY GARDEN

SET A BED TIME

NO SCREEN TIME IN THE EVENINGS

WEEK# DATES: / / - / /

SETTING MY INTENTION: FOR THIS WEEK OR MONTH

FOR MORE ENERGY

/7
/7
/7
/7

FOR MY SOUL

/7
/7
/7
/7

FOR MY FITNESS

/7
/7
/7
/7

FOR FUN/LIFE BALANCE

/7
/7
/7
/7

FOR MY SUCCESS

/7
/7
/7
/7

NOTES

M T W T F S S

ACCOUNTABILITY BUDDY JOURNAL

MY FOCUS: THE MOST IMPORTANT ITEM TO COMPLETE

WEEKLY RECAP/OBSERVATIONS

WHAT DID I AVOID THIS WEEK?

WHAT DID I LEARN THIS WEEK?

WHAT AM I GRATEFUL FOR THIS WEEK?

WHO COULD I THANK THIS WEEK?

WHAT DID I ACCOMPLISH THIS WEEK THAT I'M PROUD OF?

WEEK# DATES: / / - / /

SETTING MY INTENTION: FOR THIS WEEK OR MONTH

FOR MORE ENERGY

/7
/7
/7
/7

FOR MY SOUL

/7
/7
/7
/7

FOR MY FITNESS

/7
/7
/7
/7

FOR FUN/LIFE BALANCE

/7
/7
/7
/7

FOR MY SUCCESS

/7
/7
/7
/7

NOTES   M T W T F S S

ACCOUNTABILITY BUDDY JOURNAL

MY FOCUS: THE MOST IMPORTANT ITEM TO COMPLETE

WEEKLY RECAP/OBSERVATIONS

WHAT DID I AVOID THIS WEEK?

WHAT DID I LEARN THIS WEEK?

WHAT AM I GRATEFUL FOR THIS WEEK?

WHO COULD I THANK THIS WEEK?

WHAT DID I ACCOMPLISH THIS WEEK THAT I'M PROUD OF?

WEEK#   DATES: / / -   / /

SETTING MY INTENTION: FOR THIS WEEK OR MONTH

FOR MORE ENERGY

/7
/7
/7
/7

FOR MY SOUL

/7
/7
/7
/7

FOR MY FITNESS

/7
/7
/7
/7

FOR FUN/LIFE BALANCE

/7
/7
/7
/7

FOR MY SUCCESS

/7
/7
/7
/7

NOTES   M T W T F S S

ACCOUNTABILITY BUDDY JOURNAL

MY FOCUS: THE MOST IMPORTANT ITEM TO COMPLETE

WEEKLY RECAP/OBSERVATIONS

WHAT DID I AVOID THIS WEEK?

WHAT DID I LEARN THIS WEEK?

WHAT AM I GRATEFUL FOR THIS WEEK?

WHO COULD I THANK THIS WEEK?

WHAT DID I ACCOMPLISH THIS WEEK THAT I'M PROUD OF?

WEEK# DATES: / / - / /

SETTING MY INTENTION: FOR THIS WEEK OR MONTH

FOR MORE ENERGY

/7
/7
/7
/7

FOR MY SOUL

/7
/7
/7
/7

FOR MY FITNESS

/7
/7
/7
/7

FOR FUN/LIFE BALANCE

/7
/7
/7
/7

FOR MY SUCCESS

/7
/7
/7
/7

NOTES

M T W T F S S

ACCOUNTABILITY BUDDY JOURNAL

MY FOCUS: THE MOST IMPORTANT ITEM TO COMPLETE

WEEKLY RECAP/OBSERVATIONS

WHAT DID I AVOID THIS WEEK?

WHAT DID I LEARN THIS WEEK?

WHAT AM I GRATEFUL FOR THIS WEEK?

WHO COULD I THANK THIS WEEK?

WHAT DID I ACCOMPLISH THIS WEEK THAT I'M PROUD OF?

WEEK#   DATES: / /   -   / /

SETTING MY INTENTION: FOR THIS WEEK OR MONTH

FOR MORE ENERGY

/7
/7
/7
/7

FOR MY SOUL

/7
/7
/7
/7

FOR MY FITNESS

/7
/7
/7
/7

FOR FUN/LIFE BALANCE

/7
/7
/7
/7

FOR MY SUCCESS

/7
/7
/7
/7

NOTES   M T W T F S S

ACCOUNTABILITY BUDDY JOURNAL

MY FOCUS: THE MOST IMPORTANT ITEM TO COMPLETE

WEEKLY RECAP/OBSERVATIONS

WHAT DID I AVOID THIS WEEK?

WHAT DID I LEARN THIS WEEK?

WHAT AM I GRATEFUL FOR THIS WEEK?

WHO COULD I THANK THIS WEEK?

WHAT DID I ACCOMPLISH THIS WEEK THAT I'M PROUD OF?

WEEK# DATES: / / - / /

SETTING MY INTENTION: FOR THIS WEEK OR MONTH

FOR MORE ENERGY

/7
/7
/7
/7

FOR MY SOUL

/7
/7
/7
/7

FOR MY FITNESS

/7
/7
/7
/7

FOR FUN/LIFE BALANCE

/7
/7
/7
/7

FOR MY SUCCESS

/7
/7
/7
/7

NOTES

M T W T F S S

ACCOUNTABILITY BUDDY JOURNAL

MY FOCUS: THE MOST IMPORTANT ITEM TO COMPLETE

WEEKLY RECAP/OBSERVATIONS

WHAT DID I AVOID THIS WEEK?

WHAT DID I LEARN THIS WEEK?

WHAT AM I GRATEFUL FOR THIS WEEK?

WHO COULD I THANK THIS WEEK?

WHAT DID I ACCOMPLISH THIS WEEK THAT I'M PROUD OF?

WEEK# DATES: / / - / /

SETTING MY INTENTION: FOR THIS WEEK OR MONTH

FOR MORE ENERGY

/7
/7
/7
/7

FOR MY SOUL

/7
/7
/7
/7

FOR MY FITNESS

/7
/7
/7
/7

FOR FUN/LIFE BALANCE

/7
/7
/7
/7

FOR MY SUCCESS

/7
/7
/7
/7

NOTES

M T W T F S S

ACCOUNTABILITY BUDDY JOURNAL

MY FOCUS: THE MOST IMPORTANT ITEM TO COMPLETE

WEEKLY RECAP/OBSERVATIONS

WHAT DID I AVOID THIS WEEK?

WHAT DID I LEARN THIS WEEK?

WHAT AM I GRATEFUL FOR THIS WEEK?

WHO COULD I THANK THIS WEEK?

WHAT DID I ACCOMPLISH THIS WEEK THAT I'M PROUD OF?

WEEK# DATES: / / - / /

SETTING MY INTENTION: FOR THIS WEEK OR MONTH

FOR MORE ENERGY

/7
/7
/7
/7

FOR MY SOUL

/7
/7
/7
/7

FOR MY FITNESS

/7
/7
/7
/7

FOR FUN/LIFE BALANCE

/7
/7
/7
/7

FOR MY SUCCESS

/7
/7
/7
/7

NOTES

M T W T F S S

ACCOUNTABILITY BUDDY JOURNAL

MY FOCUS: THE MOST IMPORTANT ITEM TO COMPLETE

WEEKLY RECAP/OBSERVATIONS

WHAT DID I AVOID THIS WEEK?

WHAT DID I LEARN THIS WEEK?

WHAT AM I GRATEFUL FOR THIS WEEK?

WHO COULD I THANK THIS WEEK?

WHAT DID I ACCOMPLISH THIS WEEK THAT I'M PROUD OF?

WEEK#   DATES: / / - / /

SETTING MY INTENTION: FOR THIS WEEK OR MONTH

FOR MORE ENERGY

.... /7
.... /7
.... /7
.... /7

FOR MY SOUL

.... /7
.... /7
.... /7
.... /7

FOR MY FITNESS

.... /7
.... /7
.... /7
.... /7

FOR FUN/LIFE BALANCE

.... /7
.... /7
.... /7
.... /7

FOR MY SUCCESS

.... /7
.... /7
.... /7
.... /7

NOTES   M T W T F S S

ACCOUNTABILITY BUDDY JOURNAL

MY FOCUS: THE MOST IMPORTANT ITEM TO COMPLETE

WEEKLY RECAP/OBSERVATIONS

WHAT DID I AVOID THIS WEEK?

WHAT DID I LEARN THIS WEEK?

WHAT AM I GRATEFUL FOR THIS WEEK?

WHO COULD I THANK THIS WEEK?

WHAT DID I ACCOMPLISH THIS WEEK THAT I'M PROUD OF?

WEEK# DATES: / / - / /

SETTING MY INTENTION: FOR THIS WEEK OR MONTH

FOR MORE ENERGY

/7
/7
/7
/7

FOR MY SOUL

/7
/7
/7
/7

FOR MY FITNESS

/7
/7
/7
/7

FOR FUN/LIFE BALANCE

/7
/7
/7
/7

FOR MY SUCCESS

/7
/7
/7
/7

NOTES

M T W T F S S

ACCOUNTABILITY BUDDY JOURNAL

MY FOCUS: THE MOST IMPORTANT ITEM TO COMPLETE

WEEKLY RECAP/OBSERVATIONS

WHAT DID I AVOID THIS WEEK?

WHAT DID I LEARN THIS WEEK?

WHAT AM I GRATEFUL FOR THIS WEEK?

WHO COULD I THANK THIS WEEK?

WHAT DID I ACCOMPLISH THIS WEEK THAT I'M PROUD OF?

WEEK#   DATES: / / – / /

SETTING MY INTENTION: FOR THIS WEEK OR MONTH

FOR MORE ENERGY

/7
/7
/7
/7

FOR MY SOUL

/7
/7
/7
/7

FOR MY FITNESS

/7
/7
/7
/7

FOR FUN/LIFE BALANCE

/7
/7
/7
/7

FOR MY SUCCESS

/7
/7
/7
/7

NOTES   M T W T F S S

ACCOUNTABILITY BUDDY JOURNAL

MY FOCUS: THE MOST IMPORTANT ITEM TO COMPLETE

WEEKLY RECAP/OBSERVATIONS

WHAT DID I AVOID THIS WEEK?

WHAT DID I LEARN THIS WEEK?

WHAT AM I GRATEFUL FOR THIS WEEK?

WHO COULD I THANK THIS WEEK?

WHAT DID I ACCOMPLISH THIS WEEK THAT I'M PROUD OF?

WEEK# DATES: / / - / /

SETTING MY INTENTION: FOR THIS WEEK OR MONTH

FOR MORE ENERGY

/7
/7
/7
/7

FOR MY SOUL

/7
/7
/7
/7

FOR MY FITNESS

/7
/7
/7
/7

FOR FUN/LIFE BALANCE

/7
/7
/7
/7

FOR MY SUCCESS

/7
/7
/7
/7

NOTES

M T W T F S S

ACCOUNTABILITY BUDDY JOURNAL

MY FOCUS: THE MOST IMPORTANT ITEM TO COMPLETE

WEEKLY RECAP/OBSERVATIONS

WHAT DID I AVOID THIS WEEK?

WHAT DID I LEARN THIS WEEK?

WHAT AM I GRATEFUL FOR THIS WEEK?

WHO COULD I THANK THIS WEEK?

WHAT DID I ACCOMPLISH THIS WEEK THAT I'M PROUD OF?

WEEK# DATES: / / - / /

SETTING MY INTENTION: FOR THIS WEEK OR MONTH

FOR MORE ENERGY

/7
/7
/7
/7

FOR MY SOUL

/7
/7
/7
/7

FOR MY FITNESS

/7
/7
/7
/7

FOR FUN/LIFE BALANCE

/7
/7
/7
/7

FOR MY SUCCESS

/7
/7
/7
/7

NOTES

M T W T F S S

ACCOUNTABILITY BUDDY JOURNAL

MY FOCUS: THE MOST IMPORTANT ITEM TO COMPLETE

WEEKLY RECAP/OBSERVATIONS

WHAT DID I AVOID THIS WEEK?

WHAT DID I LEARN THIS WEEK?

WHAT AM I GRATEFUL FOR THIS WEEK?

WHO COULD I THANK THIS WEEK?

WHAT DID I ACCOMPLISH THIS WEEK THAT I'M PROUD OF?

WEEK# DATES: / / - / /

SETTING MY INTENTION: FOR THIS WEEK OR MONTH

FOR MORE ENERGY

/7
/7
/7
/7

FOR MY SOUL

/7
/7
/7
/7

FOR MY FITNESS

/7
/7
/7
/7

FOR FUN/LIFE BALANCE

/7
/7
/7
/7

FOR MY SUCCESS

/7
/7
/7
/7

NOTES

M T W T F S S

ACCOUNTABILITY BUDDY JOURNAL

MY FOCUS: THE MOST IMPORTANT ITEM TO COMPLETE

WEEKLY RECAP/OBSERVATIONS

WHAT DID I AVOID THIS WEEK?

WHAT DID I LEARN THIS WEEK?

WHAT AM I GRATEFUL FOR THIS WEEK?

WHO COULD I THANK THIS WEEK?

WHAT DID I ACCOMPLISH THIS WEEK THAT I'M PROUD OF?

WEEK# DATES: / / - / /

SETTING MY INTENTION: FOR THIS WEEK OR MONTH

FOR MORE ENERGY

/7
/7
/7
/7

FOR MY SOUL

/7
/7
/7
/7

FOR MY FITNESS

/7
/7
/7
/7

FOR FUN/LIFE BALANCE

/7
/7
/7
/7

FOR MY SUCCESS

/7
/7
/7
/7

NOTES   M T W T F S S

ACCOUNTABILITY BUDDY JOURNAL

MY FOCUS: THE MOST IMPORTANT ITEM TO COMPLETE

WEEKLY RECAP/OBSERVATIONS

WHAT DID I AVOID THIS WEEK?

WHAT DID I LEARN THIS WEEK?

WHAT AM I GRATEFUL FOR THIS WEEK?

WHO COULD I THANK THIS WEEK?

WHAT DID I ACCOMPLISH THIS WEEK THAT I'M PROUD OF?

WEEK# DATES: / / - / /

SETTING MY INTENTION: FOR THIS WEEK OR MONTH

FOR MORE ENERGY

/7
/7
/7
/7

FOR MY SOUL

/7
/7
/7
/7

FOR MY FITNESS

/7
/7
/7
/7

FOR FUN/LIFE BALANCE

/7
/7
/7
/7

FOR MY SUCCESS

/7
/7
/7
/7

NOTES

M T W T F S S

ACCOUNTABILITY BUDDY JOURNAL

MY FOCUS: THE MOST IMPORTANT ITEM TO COMPLETE

WEEKLY RECAP/OBSERVATIONS

WHAT DID I AVOID THIS WEEK?

WHAT DID I LEARN THIS WEEK?

WHAT AM I GRATEFUL FOR THIS WEEK?

WHO COULD I THANK THIS WEEK?

WHAT DID I ACCOMPLISH THIS WEEK THAT I'M PROUD OF?

WEEK# DATES: / / - / /

SETTING MY INTENTION: FOR THIS WEEK OR MONTH

FOR MORE ENERGY

.... /7
.... /7
.... /7
.... /7

FOR MY SOUL

.... /7
.... /7
.... /7
.... /7

FOR MY FITNESS

.... /7
.... /7
.... /7
.... /7

FOR FUN/LIFE BALANCE

.... /7
.... /7
.... /7
.... /7

FOR MY SUCCESS

.... /7
.... /7
.... /7
.... /7

NOTES

M T W T F S S

ACCOUNTABILITY BUDDY JOURNAL

MY FOCUS: THE MOST IMPORTANT ITEM TO COMPLETE

WEEKLY RECAP/OBSERVATIONS

WHAT DID I AVOID THIS WEEK?

WHAT DID I LEARN THIS WEEK?

WHAT AM I GRATEFUL FOR THIS WEEK?

WHO COULD I THANK THIS WEEK?

WHAT DID I ACCOMPLISH THIS WEEK THAT I'M PROUD OF?

WEEK#   DATES: / / - / /

SETTING MY INTENTION: FOR THIS WEEK OR MONTH

FOR MORE ENERGY

/7
/7
/7
/7

FOR MY SOUL

/7
/7
/7
/7

FOR MY FITNESS

/7
/7
/7
/7

FOR FUN/LIFE BALANCE

/7
/7
/7
/7

FOR MY SUCCESS

/7
/7
/7
/7

NOTES

M T W T F S S

ACCOUNTABILITY BUDDY JOURNAL

MY FOCUS: THE MOST IMPORTANT ITEM TO COMPLETE

WEEKLY RECAP/OBSERVATIONS

WHAT DID I AVOID THIS WEEK?

WHAT DID I LEARN THIS WEEK?

WHAT AM I GRATEFUL FOR THIS WEEK?

WHO COULD I THANK THIS WEEK?

WHAT DID I ACCOMPLISH THIS WEEK THAT I'M PROUD OF?

WEEK# DATES: / / - / /

SETTING MY INTENTION: FOR THIS WEEK OR MONTH

FOR MORE ENERGY

/7
/7
/7
/7

FOR MY SOUL

/7
/7
/7
/7

FOR MY FITNESS

/7
/7
/7
/7

FOR FUN/LIFE BALANCE

/7
/7
/7
/7

FOR MY SUCCESS

/7
/7
/7
/7

NOTES   M T W T F S S

ACCOUNTABILITY BUDDY JOURNAL

MY FOCUS: THE MOST IMPORTANT ITEM TO COMPLETE

WEEKLY RECAP/OBSERVATIONS

WHAT DID I AVOID THIS WEEK?

WHAT DID I LEARN THIS WEEK?

WHAT AM I GRATEFUL FOR THIS WEEK?

WHO COULD I THANK THIS WEEK?

WHAT DID I ACCOMPLISH THIS WEEK THAT I'M PROUD OF?

WEEK# DATES: / / - / /

SETTING MY INTENTION: FOR THIS WEEK OR MONTH

FOR MORE ENERGY

/7
/7
/7
/7

FOR MY SOUL

/7
/7
/7
/7

FOR MY FITNESS

/7
/7
/7
/7

FOR FUN/LIFE BALANCE

/7
/7
/7
/7

FOR MY SUCCESS

/7
/7
/7
/7

NOTES

M T W T F S S

ACCOUNTABILITY BUDDY JOURNAL

MY FOCUS: THE MOST IMPORTANT ITEM TO COMPLETE

WEEKLY RECAP/OBSERVATIONS

WHAT DID I AVOID THIS WEEK?

WHAT DID I LEARN THIS WEEK?

WHAT AM I GRATEFUL FOR THIS WEEK?

WHO COULD I THANK THIS WEEK?

WHAT DID I ACCOMPLISH THIS WEEK THAT I'M PROUD OF?

WEEK# DATES: / / - / /

SETTING MY INTENTION: FOR THIS WEEK OR MONTH

FOR MORE ENERGY

/7

/7

/7

/7

FOR MY SOUL

/7

/7

/7

/7

FOR MY FITNESS

/7

/7

/7

/7

FOR FUN/LIFE BALANCE

/7

/7

/7

/7

FOR MY SUCCESS

/7

/7

/7

/7

NOTES

M T W T F S S

ACCOUNTABILITY BUDDY JOURNAL

MY FOCUS: THE MOST IMPORTANT ITEM TO COMPLETE

WEEKLY RECAP/OBSERVATIONS

WHAT DID I AVOID THIS WEEK?

WHAT DID I LEARN THIS WEEK?

WHAT AM I GRATEFUL FOR THIS WEEK?

WHO COULD I THANK THIS WEEK?

WHAT DID I ACCOMPLISH THIS WEEK THAT I'M PROUD OF?

WEEK# DATES: / / - / /

SETTING MY INTENTION: FOR THIS WEEK OR MONTH

FOR MORE ENERGY

/7
/7
/7
/7

FOR MY SOUL

/7
/7
/7
/7

FOR MY FITNESS

/7
/7
/7
/7

FOR FUN/LIFE BALANCE

/7
/7
/7
/7

FOR MY SUCCESS

/7
/7
/7
/7

NOTES   M T W T F S S

ACCOUNTABILITY BUDDY JOURNAL

MY FOCUS: THE MOST IMPORTANT ITEM TO COMPLETE

WEEKLY RECAP/OBSERVATIONS

WHAT DID I AVOID THIS WEEK?

WHAT DID I LEARN THIS WEEK?

WHAT AM I GRATEFUL FOR THIS WEEK?

WHO COULD I THANK THIS WEEK?

WHAT DID I ACCOMPLISH THIS WEEK THAT I'M PROUD OF?

WEEK# DATES: / / - / /

SETTING MY INTENTION: FOR THIS WEEK OR MONTH

FOR MORE ENERGY

/7
/7
/7
/7

FOR MY SOUL

/7
/7
/7
/7

FOR MY FITNESS

/7
/7
/7
/7

FOR FUN/LIFE BALANCE

/7
/7
/7
/7

FOR MY SUCCESS

/7
/7
/7
/7

NOTES

M T W T F S S

ACCOUNTABILITY BUDDY JOURNAL

MY FOCUS: THE MOST IMPORTANT ITEM TO COMPLETE

WEEKLY RECAP/OBSERVATIONS

WHAT DID I AVOID THIS WEEK?

WHAT DID I LEARN THIS WEEK?

WHAT AM I GRATEFUL FOR THIS WEEK?

WHO COULD I THANK THIS WEEK?

WHAT DID I ACCOMPLISH THIS WEEK THAT I'M PROUD OF?

WEEK# DATES: / / - / /

SETTING MY INTENTION: FOR THIS WEEK OR MONTH

FOR MORE ENERGY

/7
/7
/7
/7

FOR MY SOUL

/7
/7
/7
/7

FOR MY FITNESS

/7
/7
/7
/7

FOR FUN/LIFE BALANCE

/7
/7
/7
/7

FOR MY SUCCESS

/7
/7
/7
/7

NOTES   M T W T F S S

ACCOUNTABILITY BUDDY JOURNAL

MY FOCUS: THE MOST IMPORTANT ITEM TO COMPLETE

WEEKLY RECAP/OBSERVATIONS

WHAT DID I AVOID THIS WEEK?

WHAT DID I LEARN THIS WEEK?

WHAT AM I GRATEFUL FOR THIS WEEK?

WHO COULD I THANK THIS WEEK?

WHAT DID I ACCOMPLISH THIS WEEK THAT I'M PROUD OF?

WEEK# DATES: / / - / /

SETTING MY INTENTION: FOR THIS WEEK OR MONTH

FOR MORE ENERGY

/7
/7
/7
/7

FOR MY SOUL

/7
/7
/7
/7

FOR MY FITNESS

/7
/7
/7
/7

FOR FUN/LIFE BALANCE

/7
/7
/7
/7

FOR MY SUCCESS

/7
/7
/7
/7

NOTES   M T W T F S S

ACCOUNTABILITY BUDDY JOURNAL

MY FOCUS: THE MOST IMPORTANT ITEM TO COMPLETE

WEEKLY RECAP/OBSERVATIONS

WHAT DID I AVOID THIS WEEK?

WHAT DID I LEARN THIS WEEK?

WHAT AM I GRATEFUL FOR THIS WEEK?

WHO COULD I THANK THIS WEEK?

WHAT DID I ACCOMPLISH THIS WEEK THAT I'M PROUD OF?

WEEK# DATES: / / - / /

SETTING MY INTENTION: FOR THIS WEEK OR MONTH

FOR MORE ENERGY

/7
/7
/7
/7

FOR MY SOUL

/7
/7
/7
/7

FOR MY FITNESS

/7
/7
/7
/7

FOR FUN/LIFE BALANCE

/7
/7
/7
/7

FOR MY SUCCESS

/7
/7
/7
/7

NOTES   M T W T F S S

ACCOUNTABILITY BUDDY JOURNAL

MY FOCUS: THE MOST IMPORTANT ITEM TO COMPLETE

WEEKLY RECAP/OBSERVATIONS

WHAT DID I AVOID THIS WEEK?

WHAT DID I LEARN THIS WEEK?

WHAT AM I GRATEFUL FOR THIS WEEK?

WHO COULD I THANK THIS WEEK?

WHAT DID I ACCOMPLISH THIS WEEK THAT I'M PROUD OF?

WEEK# DATES: / / - / /

SETTING MY INTENTION: FOR THIS WEEK OR MONTH

FOR MORE ENERGY

/7
/7
/7
/7

FOR MY SOUL

/7
/7
/7
/7

FOR MY FITNESS

/7
/7
/7
/7

FOR FUN/LIFE BALANCE

/7
/7
/7
/7

FOR MY SUCCESS

/7
/7
/7
/7

NOTES   M T W T F S S

ACCOUNTABILITY BUDDY JOURNAL

MY FOCUS: THE MOST IMPORTANT ITEM TO COMPLETE

WEEKLY RECAP/OBSERVATIONS

WHAT DID I AVOID THIS WEEK?

WHAT DID I LEARN THIS WEEK?

WHAT AM I GRATEFUL FOR THIS WEEK?

WHO COULD I THANK THIS WEEK?

WHAT DID I ACCOMPLISH THIS WEEK THAT I'M PROUD OF?

WEEK# DATES: / / - / /

SETTING MY INTENTION: FOR THIS WEEK OR MONTH

FOR MORE ENERGY

/7
/7
/7
/7

FOR MY SOUL

/7
/7
/7
/7

FOR MY FITNESS

/7
/7
/7
/7

FOR FUN/LIFE BALANCE

/7
/7
/7
/7

FOR MY SUCCESS

/7
/7
/7
/7

NOTES   M T W T F S S

ACCOUNTABILITY BUDDY JOURNAL

MY FOCUS: THE MOST IMPORTANT ITEM TO COMPLETE

WEEKLY RECAP/OBSERVATIONS

WHAT DID I AVOID THIS WEEK?

WHAT DID I LEARN THIS WEEK?

WHAT AM I GRATEFUL FOR THIS WEEK?

WHO COULD I THANK THIS WEEK?

WHAT DID I ACCOMPLISH THIS WEEK THAT I'M PROUD OF?

WEEK# DATES: / / - / /

SETTING MY INTENTION: FOR THIS WEEK OR MONTH

FOR MORE ENERGY

/7
/7
/7
/7

FOR MY SOUL

/7
/7
/7
/7

FOR MY FITNESS

/7
/7
/7
/7

FOR FUN/LIFE BALANCE

/7
/7
/7
/7

FOR MY SUCCESS

/7
/7
/7
/7

NOTES

M T W T F S S

ACCOUNTABILITY BUDDY JOURNAL

MY FOCUS: THE MOST IMPORTANT ITEM TO COMPLETE

WEEKLY RECAP/OBSERVATIONS

WHAT DID I AVOID THIS WEEK?

WHAT DID I LEARN THIS WEEK?

WHAT AM I GRATEFUL FOR THIS WEEK?

WHO COULD I THANK THIS WEEK?

WHAT DID I ACCOMPLISH THIS WEEK THAT I'M PROUD OF?

WEEK# DATES: / / - / /

SETTING MY INTENTION: FOR THIS WEEK OR MONTH

FOR MORE ENERGY

/7
/7
/7
/7

FOR MY SOUL

/7
/7
/7
/7

FOR MY FITNESS

/7
/7
/7
/7

FOR FUN/LIFE BALANCE

/7
/7
/7
/7

FOR MY SUCCESS

/7
/7
/7
/7

NOTES

M T W T F S S

ACCOUNTABILITY BUDDY JOURNAL

MY FOCUS: THE MOST IMPORTANT ITEM TO COMPLETE

WEEKLY RECAP/OBSERVATIONS

WHAT DID I AVOID THIS WEEK?

WHAT DID I LEARN THIS WEEK?

WHAT AM I GRATEFUL FOR THIS WEEK?

WHO COULD I THANK THIS WEEK?

WHAT DID I ACCOMPLISH THIS WEEK THAT I'M PROUD OF?

WEEK# DATES: / / - / /

SETTING MY INTENTION: FOR THIS WEEK OR MONTH

FOR MORE ENERGY

/7
/7
/7
/7

FOR MY SOUL

/7
/7
/7
/7

FOR MY FITNESS

/7
/7
/7
/7

FOR FUN/LIFE BALANCE

/7
/7
/7
/7

FOR MY SUCCESS

/7
/7
/7
/7

NOTES

M T W T F S S

ACCOUNTABILITY BUDDY JOURNAL

MY FOCUS: THE MOST IMPORTANT ITEM TO COMPLETE

WEEKLY RECAP/OBSERVATIONS

WHAT DID I AVOID THIS WEEK?

WHAT DID I LEARN THIS WEEK?

WHAT AM I GRATEFUL FOR THIS WEEK?

WHO COULD I THANK THIS WEEK?

WHAT DID I ACCOMPLISH THIS WEEK THAT I'M PROUD OF?

WEEK# DATES: / / - / /

SETTING MY INTENTION: FOR THIS WEEK OR MONTH

FOR MORE ENERGY

/7
/7
/7
/7

FOR MY SOUL

/7
/7
/7
/7

FOR MY FITNESS

/7
/7
/7
/7

FOR FUN/LIFE BALANCE

/7
/7
/7
/7

FOR MY SUCCESS

/7
/7
/7
/7

NOTES

M T W T F S S

ACCOUNTABILITY BUDDY JOURNAL

MY FOCUS: THE MOST IMPORTANT ITEM TO COMPLETE

WEEKLY RECAP/OBSERVATIONS

WHAT DID I AVOID THIS WEEK?

WHAT DID I LEARN THIS WEEK?

WHAT AM I GRATEFUL FOR THIS WEEK?

WHO COULD I THANK THIS WEEK?

WHAT DID I ACCOMPLISH THIS WEEK THAT I'M PROUD OF?

WEEK# DATES: / / - / /

SETTING MY INTENTION: FOR THIS WEEK OR MONTH

FOR MORE ENERGY

/7
/7
/7
/7

FOR MY SOUL

/7
/7
/7
/7

FOR MY FITNESS

/7
/7
/7
/7

FOR FUN/LIFE BALANCE

/7
/7
/7
/7

FOR MY SUCCESS

/7
/7
/7
/7

NOTES   M T W T F S S

ACCOUNTABILITY BUDDY JOURNAL

MY FOCUS: THE MOST IMPORTANT ITEM TO COMPLETE

WEEKLY RECAP/OBSERVATIONS

WHAT DID I AVOID THIS WEEK?

WHAT DID I LEARN THIS WEEK?

WHAT AM I GRATEFUL FOR THIS WEEK?

WHO COULD I THANK THIS WEEK?

WHAT DID I ACCOMPLISH THIS WEEK THAT I'M PROUD OF?

WEEK# DATES: / / - / /

SETTING MY INTENTION: FOR THIS WEEK OR MONTH

FOR MORE ENERGY

/7
/7
/7
/7

FOR MY SOUL

/7
/7
/7
/7

FOR MY FITNESS

/7
/7
/7
/7

FOR FUN/LIFE BALANCE

/7
/7
/7
/7

FOR MY SUCCESS

/7
/7
/7
/7

NOTES   M T W T F S S

ACCOUNTABILITY BUDDY JOURNAL

MY FOCUS: THE MOST IMPORTANT ITEM TO COMPLETE

WEEKLY RECAP/OBSERVATIONS

WHAT DID I AVOID THIS WEEK?

WHAT DID I LEARN THIS WEEK?

WHAT AM I GRATEFUL FOR THIS WEEK?

WHO COULD I THANK THIS WEEK?

WHAT DID I ACCOMPLISH THIS WEEK THAT I'M PROUD OF?

WEEK# DATES: / / - / /

SETTING MY INTENTION: FOR THIS WEEK OR MONTH

FOR MORE ENERGY

/7
/7
/7
/7

FOR MY SOUL

/7
/7
/7
/7

FOR MY FITNESS

/7
/7
/7
/7

FOR FUN/LIFE BALANCE

/7
/7
/7
/7

FOR MY SUCCESS

/7
/7
/7
/7

NOTES   M T W T F S S

ACCOUNTABILITY BUDDY JOURNAL

MY FOCUS: THE MOST IMPORTANT ITEM TO COMPLETE

WEEKLY RECAP/OBSERVATIONS

WHAT DID I AVOID THIS WEEK?

WHAT DID I LEARN THIS WEEK?

WHAT AM I GRATEFUL FOR THIS WEEK?

WHO COULD I THANK THIS WEEK?

WHAT DID I ACCOMPLISH THIS WEEK THAT I'M PROUD OF?

WEEK#   DATES: / /   -   / /

SETTING MY INTENTION: FOR THIS WEEK OR MONTH

FOR MORE ENERGY

.... /7
.... /7
.... /7
.... /7

FOR MY SOUL

.... /7
.... /7
.... /7
.... /7

FOR MY FITNESS

.... /7
.... /7
.... /7
.... /7

FOR FUN/LIFE BALANCE

.... /7
.... /7
.... /7
.... /7

FOR MY SUCCESS

.... /7
.... /7
.... /7
.... /7

NOTES   M T W T F S S

ACCOUNTABILITY BUDDY JOURNAL

MY FOCUS: THE MOST IMPORTANT ITEM TO COMPLETE

WEEKLY RECAP/OBSERVATIONS

WHAT DID I AVOID THIS WEEK?

WHAT DID I LEARN THIS WEEK?

WHAT AM I GRATEFUL FOR THIS WEEK?

WHO COULD I THANK THIS WEEK?

WHAT DID I ACCOMPLISH THIS WEEK THAT I'M PROUD OF?

WEEK# DATES: / / - / /

SETTING MY INTENTION: FOR THIS WEEK OR MONTH

FOR MORE ENERGY

/7
/7
/7
/7

FOR MY SOUL

/7
/7
/7
/7

FOR MY FITNESS

/7
/7
/7
/7

FOR FUN/LIFE BALANCE

/7
/7
/7
/7

FOR MY SUCCESS

/7
/7
/7
/7

NOTES

M T W T F S S

ACCOUNTABILITY BUDDY JOURNAL

MY FOCUS: THE MOST IMPORTANT ITEM TO COMPLETE

WEEKLY RECAP/OBSERVATIONS

WHAT DID I AVOID THIS WEEK?

WHAT DID I LEARN THIS WEEK?

WHAT AM I GRATEFUL FOR THIS WEEK?

WHO COULD I THANK THIS WEEK?

WHAT DID I ACCOMPLISH THIS WEEK THAT I'M PROUD OF?

WEEK#   DATES: / / – / /

SETTING MY INTENTION: FOR THIS WEEK OR MONTH

FOR MORE ENERGY

/7
/7
/7
/7

FOR MY SOUL

/7
/7
/7
/7

FOR MY FITNESS

/7
/7
/7
/7

FOR FUN/LIFE BALANCE

/7
/7
/7
/7

FOR MY SUCCESS

/7
/7
/7
/7

NOTES   M T W T F S S

ACCOUNTABILITY BUDDY JOURNAL

MY FOCUS: THE MOST IMPORTANT ITEM TO COMPLETE

WEEKLY RECAP/OBSERVATIONS

WHAT DID I AVOID THIS WEEK?

WHAT DID I LEARN THIS WEEK?

WHAT AM I GRATEFUL FOR THIS WEEK?

WHO COULD I THANK THIS WEEK?

WHAT DID I ACCOMPLISH THIS WEEK THAT I'M PROUD OF?

WEEK# DATES: / / - / /

SETTING MY INTENTION: FOR THIS WEEK OR MONTH

FOR MORE ENERGY

/7
/7
/7
/7

FOR MY SOUL

/7
/7
/7
/7

FOR MY FITNESS

/7
/7
/7
/7

FOR FUN/LIFE BALANCE

/7
/7
/7
/7

FOR MY SUCCESS

/7
/7
/7
/7

NOTES   M T W T F S S

ACCOUNTABILITY BUDDY JOURNAL

MY FOCUS: THE MOST IMPORTANT ITEM TO COMPLETE

WEEKLY RECAP/OBSERVATIONS

WHAT DID I AVOID THIS WEEK?

WHAT DID I LEARN THIS WEEK?

WHAT AM I GRATEFUL FOR THIS WEEK?

WHO COULD I THANK THIS WEEK?

WHAT DID I ACCOMPLISH THIS WEEK THAT I'M PROUD OF?

WEEK# DATES: / / - / /

SETTING MY INTENTION: FOR THIS WEEK OR MONTH

FOR MORE ENERGY

/7
/7
/7
/7

FOR MY SOUL

/7
/7
/7
/7

FOR MY FITNESS

/7
/7
/7
/7

FOR FUN/LIFE BALANCE

/7
/7
/7
/7

FOR MY SUCCESS

/7
/7
/7
/7

NOTES   M T W T F S S

ACCOUNTABILITY BUDDY JOURNAL

MY FOCUS: THE MOST IMPORTANT ITEM TO COMPLETE

WEEKLY RECAP/OBSERVATIONS

WHAT DID I AVOID THIS WEEK?

WHAT DID I LEARN THIS WEEK?

WHAT AM I GRATEFUL FOR THIS WEEK?

WHO COULD I THANK THIS WEEK?

WHAT DID I ACCOMPLISH THIS WEEK THAT I'M PROUD OF?

WEEK#   DATES: / / -   / /

SETTING MY INTENTION: FOR THIS WEEK OR MONTH

FOR MORE ENERGY

/7
/7
/7
/7

FOR MY SOUL

/7
/7
/7
/7

FOR MY FITNESS

/7
/7
/7
/7

FOR FUN/LIFE BALANCE

/7
/7
/7
/7

FOR MY SUCCESS

/7
/7
/7
/7

NOTES   M T W T F S S

ACCOUNTABILITY BUDDY JOURNAL

MY FOCUS: THE MOST IMPORTANT ITEM TO COMPLETE

WEEKLY RECAP/OBSERVATIONS

WHAT DID I AVOID THIS WEEK?

WHAT DID I LEARN THIS WEEK?

WHAT AM I GRATEFUL FOR THIS WEEK?

WHO COULD I THANK THIS WEEK?

WHAT DID I ACCOMPLISH THIS WEEK THAT I'M PROUD OF?

WEEK# DATES: / / - / /

SETTING MY INTENTION: FOR THIS WEEK OR MONTH

FOR MORE ENERGY

/7
/7
/7
/7

FOR MY SOUL

/7
/7
/7
/7

FOR MY FITNESS

/7
/7
/7
/7

FOR FUN/LIFE BALANCE

/7
/7
/7
/7

FOR MY SUCCESS

/7
/7
/7
/7

NOTES   M T W T F S S

ACCOUNTABILITY BUDDY JOURNAL

MY FOCUS: THE MOST IMPORTANT ITEM TO COMPLETE

WEEKLY RECAP/OBSERVATIONS

WHAT DID I AVOID THIS WEEK?

WHAT DID I LEARN THIS WEEK?

WHAT AM I GRATEFUL FOR THIS WEEK?

WHO COULD I THANK THIS WEEK?

WHAT DID I ACCOMPLISH THIS WEEK THAT I'M PROUD OF?

WEEK# DATES: / / - / /

SETTING MY INTENTION: FOR THIS WEEK OR MONTH

FOR MORE ENERGY

/7
/7
/7
/7

FOR MY SOUL

/7
/7
/7
/7

FOR MY FITNESS

/7
/7
/7
/7

FOR FUN/LIFE BALANCE

/7
/7
/7
/7

FOR MY SUCCESS

/7
/7
/7
/7

NOTES   M T W T F S S

ACCOUNTABILITY BUDDY JOURNAL

MY FOCUS: THE MOST IMPORTANT ITEM TO COMPLETE

WEEKLY RECAP/OBSERVATIONS

WHAT DID I AVOID THIS WEEK?

WHAT DID I LEARN THIS WEEK?

WHAT AM I GRATEFUL FOR THIS WEEK?

WHO COULD I THANK THIS WEEK?

WHAT DID I ACCOMPLISH THIS WEEK THAT I'M PROUD OF?

WEEK# DATES: / / - / /

SETTING MY INTENTION: FOR THIS WEEK OR MONTH

FOR MORE ENERGY

/7
/7
/7
/7

FOR MY SOUL

/7
/7
/7
/7

FOR MY FITNESS

/7
/7
/7
/7

FOR FUN/LIFE BALANCE

/7
/7
/7
/7

FOR MY SUCCESS

/7
/7
/7
/7

NOTES

M T W T F S S

ACCOUNTABILITY BUDDY JOURNAL

MY FOCUS: THE MOST IMPORTANT ITEM TO COMPLETE

WEEKLY RECAP/OBSERVATIONS

WHAT DID I AVOID THIS WEEK?

WHAT DID I LEARN THIS WEEK?

WHAT AM I GRATEFUL FOR THIS WEEK?

WHO COULD I THANK THIS WEEK?

WHAT DID I ACCOMPLISH THIS WEEK THAT I'M PROUD OF?

WEEK# DATES: / / - / /

SETTING MY INTENTION: FOR THIS WEEK OR MONTH

FOR MORE ENERGY

/7
/7
/7
/7

FOR MY SOUL

/7
/7
/7
/7

FOR MY FITNESS

/7
/7
/7
/7

FOR FUN/LIFE BALANCE

/7
/7
/7
/7

FOR MY SUCCESS

/7
/7
/7
/7

NOTES

M T W T F S S

ACCOUNTABILITY BUDDY JOURNAL

MY FOCUS: THE MOST IMPORTANT ITEM TO COMPLETE

WEEKLY RECAP/OBSERVATIONS

WHAT DID I AVOID THIS WEEK?

WHAT DID I LEARN THIS WEEK?

WHAT AM I GRATEFUL FOR THIS WEEK?

WHO COULD I THANK THIS WEEK?

WHAT DID I ACCOMPLISH THIS WEEK THAT I'M PROUD OF?

WEEK#   DATES: / / - / /

SETTING MY INTENTION: FOR THIS WEEK OR MONTH

FOR MORE ENERGY

/7

/7

/7

/7

FOR MY SOUL

/7

/7

/7

/7

FOR MY FITNESS

/7

/7

/7

/7

FOR FUN/LIFE BALANCE

/7

/7

/7

/7

FOR MY SUCCESS

/7

/7

/7

/7

NOTES   M T W T F S S

ACCOUNTABILITY BUDDY JOURNAL

MY FOCUS: THE MOST IMPORTANT ITEM TO COMPLETE

WEEKLY RECAP/OBSERVATIONS

WHAT DID I AVOID THIS WEEK?

WHAT DID I LEARN THIS WEEK?

WHAT AM I GRATEFUL FOR THIS WEEK?

WHO COULD I THANK THIS WEEK?

WHAT DID I ACCOMPLISH THIS WEEK THAT I'M PROUD OF?

WEEK# DATES: / / - / /

SETTING MY INTENTION: FOR THIS WEEK OR MONTH

FOR MORE ENERGY

/7
/7
/7
/7

FOR MY SOUL

/7
/7
/7
/7

FOR MY FITNESS

/7
/7
/7
/7

FOR FUN/LIFE BALANCE

/7
/7
/7
/7

FOR MY SUCCESS

/7
/7
/7
/7

NOTES

M T W T F S S

ACCOUNTABILITY BUDDY JOURNAL

MY FOCUS: THE MOST IMPORTANT ITEM TO COMPLETE

WEEKLY RECAP/OBSERVATIONS

WHAT DID I AVOID THIS WEEK?

WHAT DID I LEARN THIS WEEK?

WHAT AM I GRATEFUL FOR THIS WEEK?

WHO COULD I THANK THIS WEEK?

WHAT DID I ACCOMPLISH THIS WEEK THAT I'M PROUD OF?

WEEK# DATES: / / - / /

SETTING MY INTENTION: FOR THIS WEEK OR MONTH

FOR MORE ENERGY

/7
/7
/7
/7

FOR MY SOUL

/7
/7
/7
/7

FOR MY FITNESS

/7
/7
/7
/7

FOR FUN/LIFE BALANCE

/7
/7
/7
/7

FOR MY SUCCESS

/7
/7
/7
/7

NOTES   M T W T F S S

ACCOUNTABILITY BUDDY JOURNAL

MY FOCUS: THE MOST IMPORTANT ITEM TO COMPLETE

WEEKLY RECAP/OBSERVATIONS

WHAT DID I AVOID THIS WEEK?

WHAT DID I LEARN THIS WEEK?

WHAT AM I GRATEFUL FOR THIS WEEK?

WHO COULD I THANK THIS WEEK?

WHAT DID I ACCOMPLISH THIS WEEK THAT I'M PROUD OF?

WEEK# DATES: / / — / /

SETTING MY INTENTION: FOR THIS WEEK OR MONTH

FOR MORE ENERGY

/7
/7
/7
/7

FOR MY SOUL

/7
/7
/7
/7

FOR MY FITNESS

/7
/7
/7
/7

FOR FUN/LIFE BALANCE

/7
/7
/7
/7

FOR MY SUCCESS

/7
/7
/7
/7

NOTES

M T W T F S S

ACCOUNTABILITY BUDDY JOURNAL

MY FOCUS: THE MOST IMPORTANT ITEM TO COMPLETE

WEEKLY RECAP/OBSERVATIONS

WHAT DID I AVOID THIS WEEK?

WHAT DID I LEARN THIS WEEK?

WHAT AM I GRATEFUL FOR THIS WEEK?

WHO COULD I THANK THIS WEEK?

WHAT DID I ACCOMPLISH THIS WEEK THAT I'M PROUD OF?

WEEK#   DATES: / / - / /

SETTING MY INTENTION: FOR THIS WEEK OR MONTH

FOR MORE ENERGY

.... /7
.... /7
.... /7
.... /7

FOR MY SOUL

.... /7
.... /7
.... /7
.... /7

FOR MY FITNESS

.... /7
.... /7
.... /7
.... /7

FOR FUN/LIFE BALANCE

.... /7
.... /7
.... /7
.... /7

FOR MY SUCCESS

.... /7
.... /7
.... /7
.... /7

NOTES

M T W T F S S

ACCOUNTABILITY BUDDY JOURNAL

MY FOCUS: THE MOST IMPORTANT ITEM TO COMPLETE

WEEKLY RECAP/OBSERVATIONS

WHAT DID I AVOID THIS WEEK?

WHAT DID I LEARN THIS WEEK?

WHAT AM I GRATEFUL FOR THIS WEEK?

WHO COULD I THANK THIS WEEK?

WHAT DID I ACCOMPLISH THIS WEEK THAT I'M PROUD OF?

WEEK#   DATES: / / - / /

SETTING MY INTENTION: FOR THIS WEEK OR MONTH

FOR MORE ENERGY

/7

/7

/7

/7

FOR MY SOUL

/7

/7

/7

/7

FOR MY FITNESS

/7

/7

/7

/7

FOR FUN/LIFE BALANCE

/7

/7

/7

/7

FOR MY SUCCESS

/7

/7

/7

/7

NOTES

M T W T F S S

ACCOUNTABILITY BUDDY JOURNAL

MY FOCUS: THE MOST IMPORTANT ITEM TO COMPLETE

WEEKLY RECAP/OBSERVATIONS

WHAT DID I AVOID THIS WEEK?

WHAT DID I LEARN THIS WEEK?

WHAT AM I GRATEFUL FOR THIS WEEK?

WHO COULD I THANK THIS WEEK?

WHAT DID I ACCOMPLISH THIS WEEK THAT I'M PROUD OF?

WEEK#   DATES: / / -   / /

SETTING MY INTENTION: FOR THIS WEEK OR MONTH

FOR MORE ENERGY

/7
/7
/7
/7

FOR MY SOUL

/7
/7
/7
/7

FOR MY FITNESS

/7
/7
/7
/7

FOR FUN/LIFE BALANCE

/7
/7
/7
/7

FOR MY SUCCESS

/7
/7
/7
/7

NOTES   M T W T F S S

ACCOUNTABILITY BUDDY JOURNAL

MY FOCUS: THE MOST IMPORTANT ITEM TO COMPLETE

WEEKLY RECAP/OBSERVATIONS

WHAT DID I AVOID THIS WEEK?

WHAT DID I LEARN THIS WEEK?

WHAT AM I GRATEFUL FOR THIS WEEK?

WHO COULD I THANK THIS WEEK?

WHAT DID I ACCOMPLISH THIS WEEK THAT I'M PROUD OF?

12 MONTH GOAL BLUEPRINT

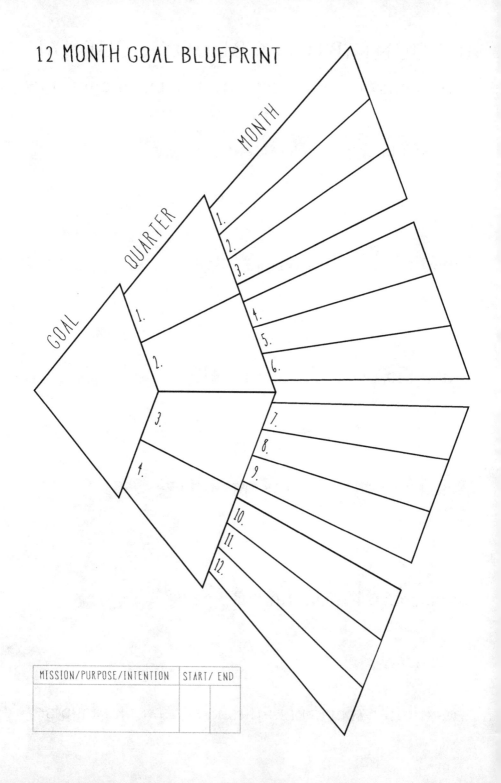

MONTH

QUARTER

GOAL

1.
2.
3.

1.

2.

4.
5.
6.

3.

4.

7.
8.
9.

10.
11.
12.

MISSION/PURPOSE/INTENTION	START/ END	

12 MONTH GOAL BLUEPRINT

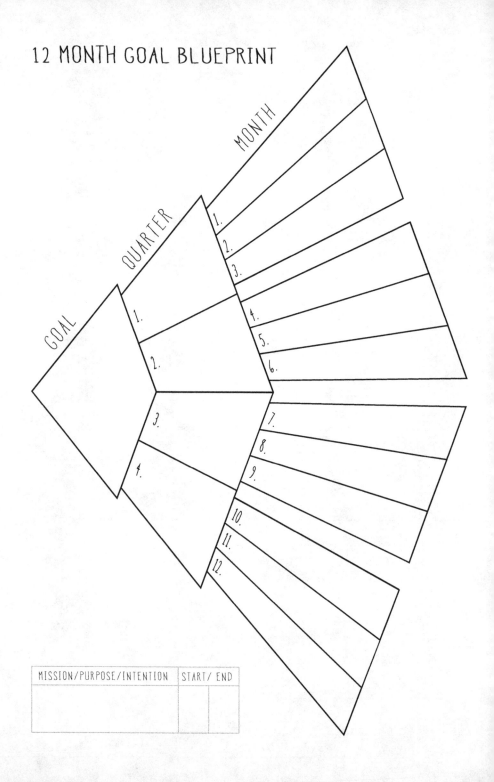

GOAL

QUARTER

MONTH

1.
2.
3.
4.

1.
2.
3.
4.
5.
6.
7.
8.
9.
10.
11.
12.

MISSION/PURPOSE/INTENTION	START/ END	

90 DAY GOAL BLUEPRINT

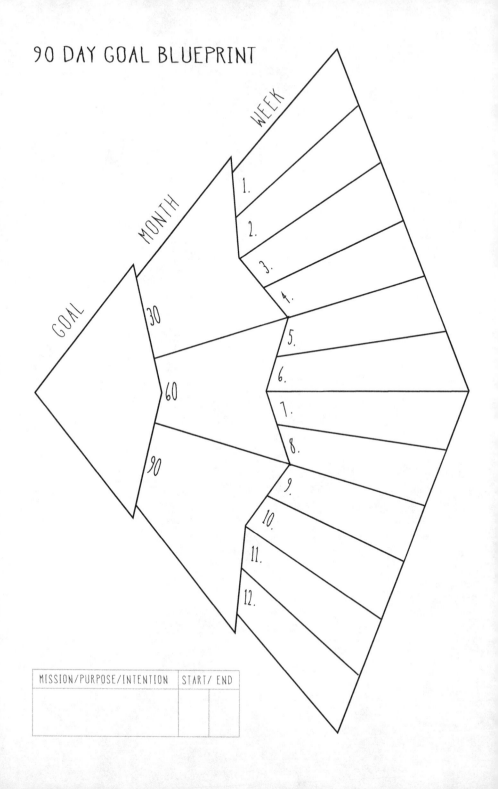

WEEK

MONTH

GOAL

1.
2.
3.
4.
5.
6.
7.
8.
9.
10.
11.
12.

30

60

90

MISSION/PURPOSE/INTENTION	START/ END	

90 DAY GOAL BLUEPRINT

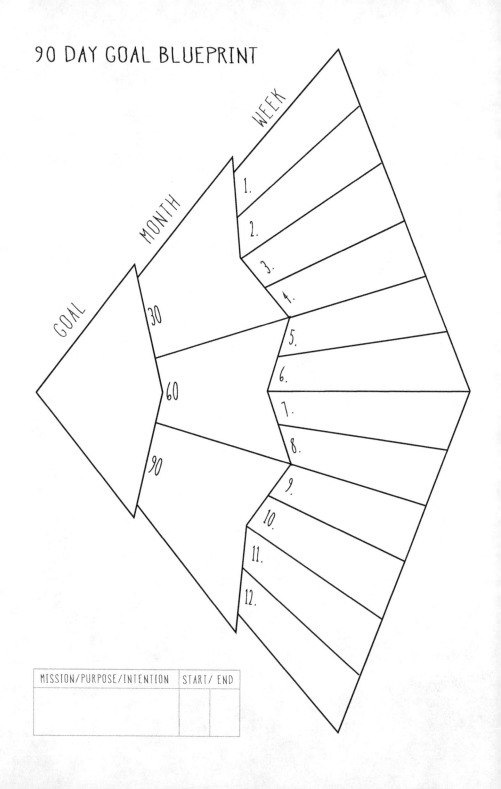

WEEK

MONTH

GOAL

1.
2.
3.
4.
5.
6.
7.
8.
9.
10.
11.
12.

30

60

90

MISSION/PURPOSE/INTENTION	START/ END	

90 DAY GOAL BLUEPRINT

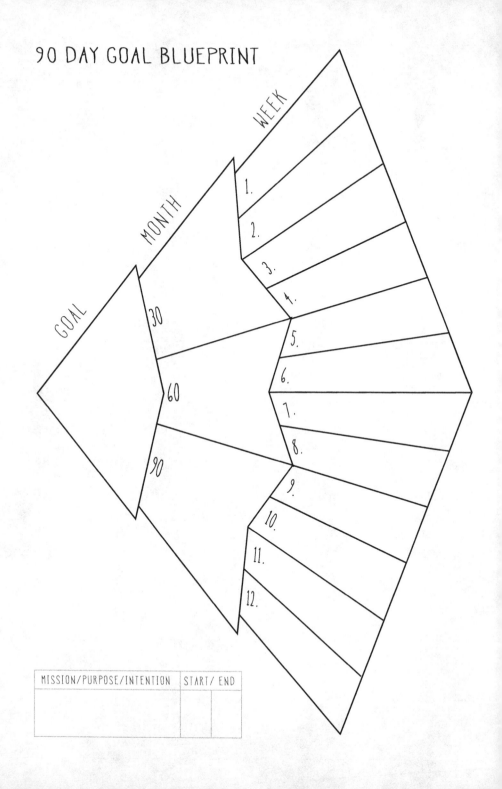

WEEK

MONTH

GOAL

1.
2.
3.
4.
5.
6.
7.
8.
9.
10.
11.
12.

30

60

90

MISSION/PURPOSE/INTENTION	START/ END	

90 DAY GOAL BLUEPRINT

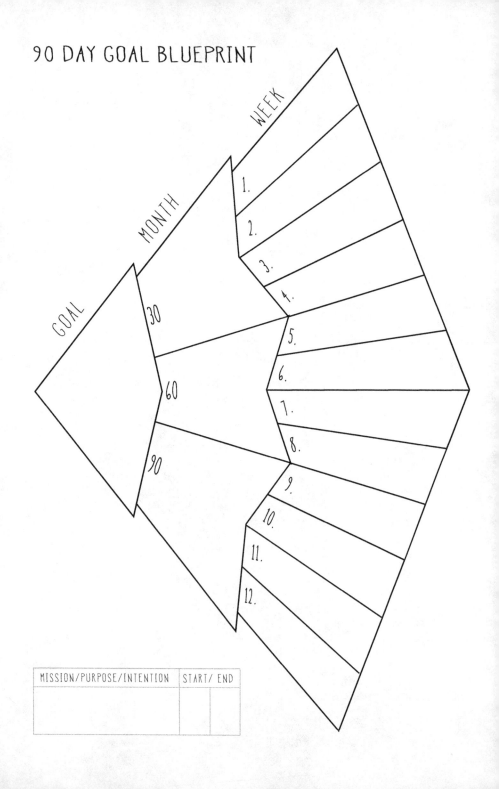

WEEK

MONTH

GOAL

1.
2.
3.
4.
5.
6.
7.
8.
9.
10.
11.
12.

30

60

90

MISSION/PURPOSE/INTENTION	START/ END	

CPSIA information can be obtained
at www.ICGtesting.com
Printed in the USA
LVHW102323080922
727935LV00013B/284